Why We Eat Grains

by Beth Bence Reinke, MS, RD

BUMBA BOOKS™

LERNER PUBLICATIONS ◆ MINNEAPOLIS

Note to Educators:

Throughout this book, you'll find critical thinking questions. These can be used to engage young readers in thinking critically about the topic and in using the text and photos to do so.

Lerner Publications Company
A division of Lerner Publishing Group, Inc.
241 First Avenue North
Minneapolis, MN 55401 USA

For reading levels and more information, look up this title at www.lernerbooks.com.

Library of Congress Cataloging–in–Publication Data

Names: Reinke, Beth Bence, author.
Title: Why we eat grains / Beth Bence Reinke, MS, RD.
Description: Minneapolis : Lerner Publications, [2018] | Series: Bumba books. Nutrition matters | Audience: Ages 4-7. | Audience: K to grade 3. | Includes bibliographical references and index.
Identifiers: LCCN 2018000236 (print) | LCCN 2017053537 (ebook) | ISBN 9781541507708 (eb pdf) | ISBN 9781541503380 (lb : alk. paper) | ISBN 9781541526846 (pb : alk. paper)
Subjects: LCSH: Grain in human nutrition--Juvenile literature. | Grain--Juvenile literature. | Nutrition--Juvenile literature.
Classification: LCC QP144.G73 (print) | LCC QP144.G73 R45 2018 (ebook) | DDC 613.2/8--dc23

LC record available at https://lccn.loc.gov/2018000236

Manufactured in the United States of America
1 – CG – 7/15/18

Table of
Contents

All about Grains

Grains give your body energy.

Did you eat grains today?

Rice and oats are grains.

Popcorn is a grain too!

Many foods are made

with grains.

Bread and cereal have

grains in them.

Nutrition Facts

Oats, whole grain, raw

Serving Size 45g/ 1/2cup dry

Amount	% Daily Value
Calories 180	
Calories from Fat 30	
Total Fat 3 g	5%
Saturated Fat 0.5 g	3%
Trans Fat	
Cholesterol 0 mg	
Sodium 0 mg	0%
Carbohydrate 29 g	0%
Fiber 5 g	10%
Sugars 1 g	19%
Protein 7 g	
Vitamin A	
Vitamin C	0%
Calcium	0%
Iron	2%
	10%

Some foods are made with only part of the grain.

Others are made with the whole grain.

Foods made with the whole grain are called whole grain foods.

Labels on foods may say *whole grain*. Can you find the words *whole grain* on this label?

We should eat mostly whole grains.

Whole grains have lots of fiber.

Where might you look to see if this cereal is a whole grain food?

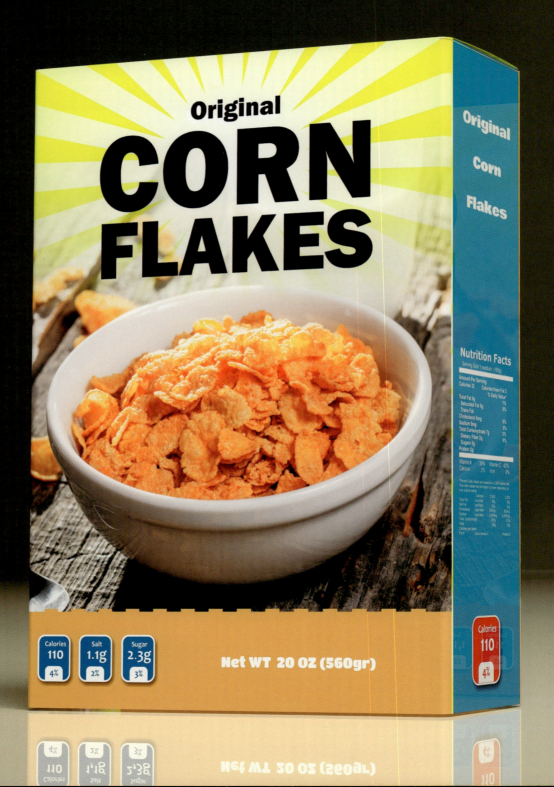

Original
CORN
FLAKES

Original

Corn

Flakes

Nutrition Facts
Serving Size 1 medium (190g)

Amount Per Serving
Calories 32   Calories from Fat 3

% Daily Value*

Total Fat 0g
Saturated Fat 0g
Trans Fat
Cholesterol 0mg
Sodium 9mg
Total Carbohydrate 7g
Dietary Fiber 7g
Sugars 5g
Protein 2g

Vitamin A   36%   Vitamin C 42%
Calcium   2%   Iron   4%

Calories	Salt	Sugar
110	1.1g	2.3g
4%	2%	3%

Net WT 20 OZ (560gr)

Calories
110
4%

Whole grains have minerals too.

Magnesium helps make your

bones strong.

Selenium helps you stay well.

B vitamins are in most grain foods.

B vitamins help your body use food for energy.

Why do you think your body needs energy?

You need five servings of grain foods

a day.

Eat oatmeal. Have a sandwich.

Eating grains helps you

stay healthy.

What are your favorite

grain foods?

20

USDA MyPlate Diagram

Fill this much of your plate with grains.

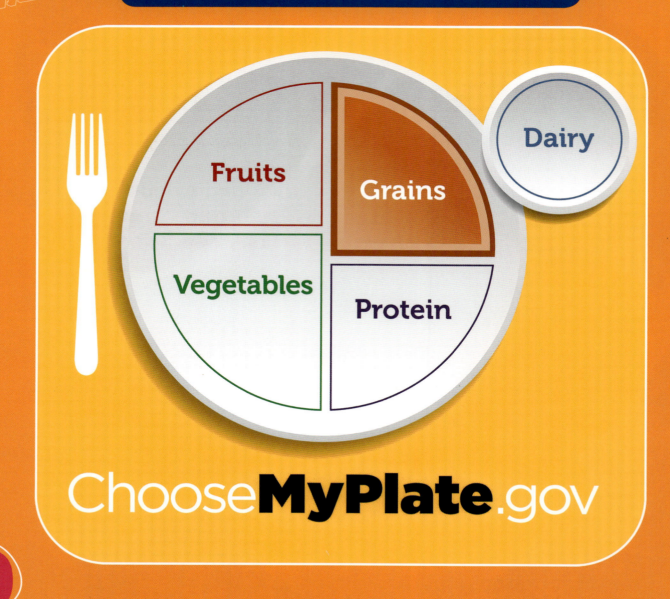

Fruits

Grains

Dairy

Vegetables

Protein

ChooseMyPlate.gov

22

Picture Glossary

fiber

the part of plant foods that the body cannot break down

minerals

nutrients such as iron, zinc, and others that your body needs for good health

vitamins

nutrients such as vitamin A, vitamin C, and others that your body needs for good health

whole grain foods

Nutrition Facts
Oats, whole grain, raw
Serving Size 45g/ 1/2cup dry

Amount	% Daily Value
Calories 180	
Calories from Fat 30	
Total Fat 3 g	5%
Saturated Fat 0.5 g	3%
Trans Fat	
Cholesterol 0 mg	0%
Sodium 0 mg	0%
Carbohydrate 29 g	10%
Fiber 5 g	19%
Sugars 1 g	
Protein 7 g	
Vitamin A	0%
Vitamin C	0%
Calcium	0%

foods made with the whole grain instead of only part of it

Read More

Black, Vanessa. *Grains*. Minneapolis: Jump!, 2017.

Clark, Rosalyn. *Why We Eat Healthy Foods*. Minneapolis: Lerner Publications, 2018.

Parker, Vic. *Grains*. Minneapolis: QEB, 2016.

Index

Photo Credits